I Cry Love! Love! Love!

I Cry Love! Love! Love!

Poems by

Randel McCraw Helms

© 2021 Randel McCraw Helms. All rights reserved.
This material may not be reproduced in any form, published,
reprinted, recorded, performed, broadcast,
rewritten or redistributed without
the explicit permission of Randel McCraw Helms.
All such actions are strictly prohibited by law.

Cover design by Shay Culligan

ISBN: 978-1-63980-039-1

Kelsay Books
502 South 1040 East, A-119
American Fork, Utah 84003
Kelsaybooks.com

For Susan
Allons!

Acknowledgments

I wish to thank the editors of the following publications, in whose pages twenty-three of these poems first appeared, sometimes in slightly different form or with different titles:

Avis: "Lament of John Thomas over Widowed Lady Jane"
Chaffin Journal: "Variations on Garcia Lorca's 'Gacela of the Terrible Presence,'" "If I Were Dead"
Coe Review: "The Glutton's Song of Love"
Dappled Things: "For His Wife, Thirty Years On"
Dove Tales: "Death Comes for St. Francis," "Bystander, near Jerusalem, Early Friday in Passover, 30 C.E."
Emeritus Voices: "If Will Hath a Will, Anne Hathaway," "After Zika: The Aborted Fetus Comforts Her Grieving Mother," "The Science of Love"
Fieldstone Review: "Potion against Heartache"
Main Street Rag: "Buttermilk," "Letter to God"
Mgversion2>Datura: "The Bridegroom Prays for Songs of Love," "Masturbation"
Pilgrim, A Journal of Catholic Experience: "Near Taos," "At a Deathbed"
Sand Canyon Review: "On Visiting His Friend, to Drink and Remember"
Sick Lit: "A Journey to Tepeyac," "Sappho Rejoices in the Fragrance of Her Beloved"
Silkworm: "Mouth These Verses," "Sooner or Later, Delicate Death"
Tipton Poetry Journal: "Found Written in the Deck of a Capsized Dinghy, near Lesbos, Summer, 2017"

Contents

Mouth These Verses	13
Found Written in the Deck of a Capsized Dinghy, near Lesbos, Summer, 2017	14
For His Wife, Thirty Years On	15
Sappho Rejoices in the Fragrance of Her Beloved	16
The Bridegroom Prays for Songs of Love	17
Potion against Heartache	18
From River-Merchants' Wives: Two Letters (After Li Po)	19
Variations on Garcia Lorca's "*Gacela* of the Terrible Presence"	21
Old, at a Drinking-Place, Late	22
A Journey to Tepeyac	23
At a Deathbed	25
At the Funeral of a Friend Who Died in Disgrace	26
On Visiting His Friend, to Drink and Remember (After Li Po)	27
The Glutton's Song of Love	28
Buttermilk	29
If Will Hath a Will, Anne Hathaway	30
Lament of John Thomas over Widowed Lady Jane	34
Revelation aboard a School Bus, Seventh Grade	35
Masturbation	36
Body My Pleasure Dome	37
"I Gave the Land a King"	38
What's the Point of Love Poetry?	40
The Science of Love	41
The Little Deaths	42
If I Were Dead	43
The Sperm of Sudan Now Sleeps in Hope	44
Near Taos	45
The Shearing of Clare by Francis	46

Death Comes for St. Francis	47
After Zika: The Aborted Fetus Comforts Her Grieving Mother	48
Sooner or Later, Delicate Death	49
Letter to God	50
Bystander, near Jerusalem, Early Friday in Passover, 30 A.D.	51

Mouth These Verses

Listen, this is no world to hunger in,
Runted and weak are early culled, squealing.
Wolf, rootle, gnaw; what cannot kill, fattens.

Just so, poems, their sharp smack vivifies:
Such feasting may swell some shriveled precincts
Unknown even to those who pasture there.

Here, I give you my dreams, the best I have.
Mouth these verses, mumble them, suck their juice;
I swear they will soothe and slipper the slide

Heavenwards of all well-greased with their love.

Found Written in the Deck of a Capsized Dinghy, near Lesbos, Summer, 2017

My name is Ali
My son's name is Muhammad
If you see my wife, whose name
Is Fatima, tell her I

For His Wife, Thirty Years On

What I can't forget is the way you kicked
Off your shoes when you came to my house
For the first time and slowly crossed the rug,
Studying pictures on the wall, and walked
Into a chair and broke your little toe.

So I knew my big hopes for later on
Were undone by pain and embarrassment,
Though I didn't mind, really, because you
Had at last arrived and liked what you saw,
And I was saying to myself, *It's her, it's her, it's her.*

Sappho Rejoices in the Fragrance of Her Beloved

My love is as a fragrant grove,
She savors of the salt of love.

The scented braid beside her ear
Loosens my knees when I draw near.

Beneath her tongue lies liquid silk,
Her breath, a waft of honeyed milk.

Below her arms, amongst the hairs,
Lies memory of foxes' lairs.

The scent of each breast is risen yeast,
Her navel, wine, a wondrous feast.

Syrups glisten her lips below,
There is, I swear, no sweeter flow,

And best of all, between her knees,
The faintest tang of ripened cheese.

The Bridegroom Prays for Songs of Love

Send me this night new songs of love,
Delicious and undiscovered melodies

To moisten and glisten her loveliness,
Rhythms to slipper the old dance,

And slow, swelling utterance
For quickening and shuddering,

To breathe upon her sweet nape and thigh
And stiffen their softest hairs erect.

Send me airs for plantation of heirs,
A brushing eyelash to tickle and swell

A reluctant, blushing, hidden nipple, bringing
Longing to open her most close, secret treasure.

Potion against Heartache

Take thee nut of hickory, root
Of chicory, parsley, parsnip and dock;
Add saffron and anise, nutmeg and thyme,
And roast it or toast it and steep it in brandy
With orris-root candy
Twelve hours straight by the clock.
To keep the taste true, fine it with rue,
Then drain it and strain it and keep it from fire;
As slowly it mellows, chill it with bellows
To coat it with frosting of rime,
Then age it in cellars like wine.
At least for a season live thee by reason,
Keep thee from sin and wagering den,
And avoid all manner of ire.
Then give thee the liquor, this magical ichor,
To pure lady whose love you desire,
And her heart shall ever be true.
Thy babies need never fear rabies nor scabies,
Scrofula, glanders, nor pox,
Just blend thee this potion into a lotion
And rub on their feeties each day.
Thy hens will all lay, thy lambkins shall play,
And give thee gold nuggets for rocks,
Thy heifers give milk, thy worms make thee silk,
All creatures shall love thee at sight,
If one gill in water thou add to their fodder
And knead it and feed it each night.

Keep thou this potion, or magical lotion,
Always beside thee no night-mare shall ride thee
No ill fate betide thee, nor eye-worm trouble thy sight.
No wife shall beshrew thee no bailiff shall rue thee
If care thou to muse thee and ever choose thee
Daily to use it aright.

From River-Merchants' Wives: Two Letters
(After Li Po)

(I)

Pulling blossoms by the tall East Gate,
My hair too short for braids,
How could I know that cloying boy
Stalking me on a thin stick-horse
And tossing green-plum stones at my head,
Would claim me, fourteen, for his own?

Given, and taken, I balked, mule,
Face to the wall unheeding, until,
Fifteen, you wakened me, you,
Whose dust I would now enfold
Upon my sleeping breast for ever
And ever and ever. So why
Must I mount this river lookout?
Sixteen, you sailed alone past Chu'Tang Gorge,
And for five months I weep beside your tracks
At the muddy Going-Out Gate; they fill
With leaves, I cannot sweep them clean.
My streaked face cakes. Even these chattering
Monkeys mourn, while I watch October's
Butterflies brightly couple around me.
How I long to see you sailing down from San-Pa!
Please, send word, I'll run to meet you,
Even as far as Long Wind Sands!

(II)

Just sixteen and almost-virgin, I kneel
By this river and plead with the wind.

At fifteen, knowing never breast-ache, gaily
I wed My Lord You in wet Chang'an spring,
Innocent of all comings and goings,
Blushing a thousand peach flowers to cleave as one
With you, for ever and ever and ever.
Then with May the south wind, and, husband, you
Sailed toward far Pa-Ling, alone. Why can you not
Return? Now long August wanes, peaches drop,
Heavy as my heart, and the west wind, I fear,
Will push you even past far Yangtzu quay,
While here, I watch paired swans delight among reeds
And flashing kingfishers cherish nestlings.
Last night a summer storm, a dream of mast-high waves,
And longing for your sweet breath on my mouth.
Please, for me, finish this long river
Business, set sail for Chang'an, and let
The north wind chill our blended flesh again.

Oh, for you, I'd mount even these swift-flowing clouds
To join just one day sooner at Blue Orchid Cove!

Variations on Garcia Lorca's "*Gacela* of the Terrible Presence"

May all these rivers flow freely to the sea,
Carving valleys for the wild and cooling storm.

May all eyes learn to pore through blackness
To every white night-sweetening bloom.

Let stolid oxen sing aloud at the manger,
And every burrowing worm find love in richest silt.

May all night-wails be soothed anew
With each bright-freshening dawn

And all dried bones be clothed again
In delicate and quivering flesh,

But most, let never setting sun bring sleep
Before I learn what fragrant darkness
Lies below that silver-buckled waist.

Old, at a Drinking-Place, Late

Half lit near midnight in this too-loud dive,
I understand the heat I feel, the warm,
Radiating thrum on cock even through denim.
I, a drinker only, old meat amid
All this youthful juice looking to gush;
Still I get it: just one small fuck, one fumble
Toward possible love, is all we need tonight.
Enough for now, we're young, and Friday-tired,
And every one of us could be beautiful
By two a.m. Then, pacing the bar like
A sweating mare, one tall hopeful approaches
Me, but quickly turns to the boy beside,
The better bet, I know, though spotty and scented
Workman-stale. Yes, it's time for me to go.

A Journey to Tepeyac

Here is recounted a grace of Our Lady
Of Guadalupe. In the village of Tepeyac,
On the very site of an ancient shrine
Sacred to Tonantzin, mother of all gods,
The Queen of the Americas blesses
All who journey here in hope and love, some
On a litter of pain, some on their bleeding knees.

In the summer of the year of our Lord
1945, the widow Lupita Jimenez fell,
Cutting her leg on a sharpened stake. The wound
Festered painfully, and, fevered, she could not rise
From her pallet, even to tend her beloved
Son, Juan Diego, or their treasured burro,
Source of their only wealth, hauling charcoal
For the village. Even as her leg refused
To heal, the burro sickened and died in
The heat. Soon centavos, then food, dwindled.

Juan Diego was strong, and lacked no love
For his mother. "Mama, what are we to do?"
"Take me to Tepeyac," she said, "to pray
Our Lady, lest we die." "But Mama,
Our burro is dead! Who can carry you?
God help me then, I will do it myself,
Though I do not know the way. Guide me."
So Juan Diego packed what food they had,
With a pallet and pillow for his mother,
Wrapping them in a strong blanket with
A large and heavy flask of water. Then
He trudged two miles toward Tepeyac and left them
Beside the path to hurry home. There, he
Hoisted his dear mother upon his back

And made his way slowly to the cache. Setting
Her gently down, he stopped to rest and drink.
Then lifting the lightening pack, he walked
Another two miles, to deposit the load
And return to his beloved mother.
This he did over ten days and sixty miles
For her, one hundred and eighty for him.

On the way, travelers who saw what love
Was here, heaped food upon them, and praises
For Juan Diego. "Go with God," they said.
During those hours, neither noticing,
The salt of the sweat of his devotion worked
Upon her wound, as slowly it healed in silence.
At Tepeyac they beheld, in awe, a clean new scar.

All saw that woman walk home with her son,
Bearing in her strong arms a sack of gifted meal.

At a Deathbed

I begged my father not to go,
But he was too busy to hear,
Intent upon the unendurable.
Dying is a grunting shove, I know,
I have watched it through a long night:
The button too much for the buttonhole,
The stickleback for the heron-throat,
The braincase for the birth canal.

Like the doomed and kicking gnu braced
On a mudbank in the toothed vise
Of a crocodile, we slip alone
Down that barbed and darkened chute
Helpless toward some mouth, knowing well
Our own slow and sweated drag
To the death rattle may stretch hours,
Gasping days, years.

At the Funeral of a Friend Who Died in Disgrace

So here is what it comes to: you must endure
This sallow lump of insincerity
Mouthing words he cannot possibly believe,
To a small, shamed crowd who do not credit
Them either, both pretending anything
Besides relief that the poor man is dead
At last and finds some peace beyond ignominy.

When you've lost a friend who had run afoul
Of law and decency in ways that you
Can scarcely imagine, what's to be done?
Worse, that he jumped from a bridge after days
Of headlines, and in front of a leering
Camera from the local news. He was your friend,
And that will stick with you like dandruff on your coat.

What do you do? You attend his funeral,
You observe the decencies at a church
You would otherwise never be seen in,
Where little girls are trained to be servile,
Members are told to vote for the despicable
And to believe risible fantasies,
Because you loved him, and because he was your friend.

On Visiting His Friend, to Drink and Remember
(After Li Po)

Descending Blue Mount by moonlight,
I turned to watch the final glow
On its snowy peak, knowing my friend's
Warm house waited in shadow below
With his good wine and welcoming hand.

His son called from the gate as I left
The tall bamboo with its clinging vines,
Eager to rejoice with a man I loved
From my youth. And there, until the dimming
Of the last bright star, we drank to the song
Of the wind in the trees, laughing together,
Telling the world and its follies to go hang.

The Glutton's Song of Love

Bathe me in ale, soak me in froth,
Give rivers of whiskey to swim in;
No time for women when rum is on tap,
And oceans of beer on the side.

Fill me with collops and gobbets of flesh,
Stay me with flagons of wine.
Give me to gnaw on glutinous gristle
And I'll belch in thankful delight.
I'd piss at the bench not to leave a feast,
And I'll die with a chop in each hand.

Send baked ham, spring lamb,
Capons skewered and hot,
With mushrooms and onions and garlic
And drippings of urinous kidney between.

Give buckets and barrels of cockles and mussels,
High-smelling meat on a spit,
Brandy fountains, chocolate mountains,
Fat biscuits with cherries on top,
And best of all, an endless supply
Of bright-colored gumdrops to suck.

May you never be empty, my belly, my god,
And my lips never whisper "Enough."

Buttermilk

Daily I crave the tart tingle of it,
The vinegar grimace of thick ferment
In curdled detritus of churn,

With savor of love in softest clabbers,
Its scent a touch of warmed crotch:
Here, my streaked beaker of salt tipple.

If Will Hath a Will, Anne Hathaway

We're in the month of August,
Fifteen eighty-two,
The weather's warm, the ground is dry;
I have a tale for you.

It's easy to imagine now
What passed near Stratford town:
The couple lay in Warwick Wood,
His hand was under her gown.

Will's a lad of eighteen year,
While Anne is twenty-six;
In country skills he's yet unversed,
But she has learned some tricks.

Anne's fast approaching spinsterhood,
While he's a healthy boy:
I can't describe specifics,
Let's simply wish them joy.

That was late in summertime;
I now pass on to fall:
Upon the house of John Shakespeare
There lay a certain pall.

He's an ambitious alderman,
While Anne is old, and rural folk;
But John, it's late to bluster now:
The sperm has pierced the yolk.

So families were reconciled,
Negotiations made,
The Banns were read but once and then
The marriage feast was laid.

The couple wed November's end,
Susannah came in May;
You, my friend, can work it out,
It happens every day.

But "happy ever after"
Cannot end this tale:
For those who wed in too much haste
Must forever ride that rail.

There's no divorce for commoners,
That's just for fat old kings;
Only Henry Number Eight
Could don six wedding rings.

Oddly now, in our own day,
We've quite reversed these tales:
Peasants can split and wed again,
But not the Prince of Wales.

At least, that is, till Princess Di
Had left the earthly scene;
But let's not enter that morass—
And now I forget where I've been.

Oh, yes. Before three summers pass,
Young Will's decamped for London town
To make his fortunes there; and, from
What I hear, he gathered real renown.

He made hit plays, and loads of cash,
Went home a time or four,
But sadly, while he was in town,
Poor Annie never passed his door.

(One Dark Lady leapt, I'm told,
Into William's empty bed;
But go and read the Sonnets, please,
And let me leap ahead.)

Three decades pass, and Will is rich;
He's bald as well, Dark Lady's gone,
And the *Globe* has burned to the ground.
Stratford calls: he'll die among his own.

Now we learn the saddest part,
If melancholy's to your taste,
Of this sad tale of honest folk
Who had to wed in haste.

Shrewish wives, or murderous,
Abandoned daughters too,
Plus his grief at Hamnet dead
Filled Will's great works, it's true;

But their unhappy wedded life
Haunts me most when I hear it said
That Will left Anne when he was dead
The second, yes the second, best bed.

Lament of John Thomas over Widowed Lady Jane

When her husband died my once-mistress called,
But I, dizzy with love for another,
Could give no help. Besides, heart said, you're bald,
Old fool, and neither is blind; why risk both?
Never trade a true one for a new one.

If only the wish could die with the strength,
Age would be sweet, calm evenings by the fire.
But lamplight and books inflame me the more,
And draw me, sweating, to the telephone.
Cunt tempts the devil, and I am evil.

Revelation aboard a School Bus, Seventh Grade

My unwelcome erection arises
Just as we approach the school, a pitiful,
Impudent little stiffie, purposeless
But to mortify a self-conscious boy.

Each grinding vibration of the downshift
Tickles it again, and then again, as we
Slow and turn at the gate; and I with no coat,
No satchel to hide it hunching down the aisle.

The bus stops, and a blushing parade awaits.
I stand, hands shielding my unrepentant member,
When at last the chastened adult slowly growing
Within me speaks up: "If you've got it, kid, own it;

What cannot be conquered must be endured."
In such moments, I learned, a saddened manhood looms.

Masturbation

Think back, think back: can you recall when it was
You first surmised, amazed, that you could place
Your hand upon a source of perfect joy,
Your very own, and always smiling there;

That you could freely summon this brilliance
At will, and with—O my!—a most finely
Fitted palm or merely single finger?
Marvelous adolescent discovery,

When farthest extremities could be made
To sing and tingle, toes to fizz and sizzle
From a rush of lovely dopamine.
(Yes, lucky youth may spend with feet as well.)

Better yet, that priests and elders darkly
Disapproved, and with grimmest helplessness.

Body My Pleasure Dome

(Homage to May Swenson)

Body my pleasure dome
What shall I do when you're not my home

When that smooth handle
I love to fondle

Has gone away I know not where
And I am made of pale blue air

Where shall I sleep
And who can I keep

As my paramour
When all I can say is Nevermore

How will it be by and by
When I'm thinner than mist in the sky

When I have no skin
In which to sin
Or pour my gin

When body my friend is gone is gone
When body my friend is gone

"I Gave the Land a King"

(As Related by Tamar, Daughter of Canaan,
Some While after Her Death: from Genesis 38)

My name was Tamar. Both my husbands died.
I had no sons, and my sad womb, unsown,
Wept red. Hear my tale, and do not judge.

Judah, son of Jacob, gave me to Er,
Yearning for heirs. But he was a sickly boy,
And could not do his duty till he died.
Judah passed me then to another son,
Married Onan, who wished no brood of me;
Every time, he withdrew before he spent,
Wasting his seed upon the barren ground.
That husband died too, and I did not grieve,
Though my lank breasts and fallow belly mourned.
I pled to Judah, "Give me sons, or I shall die,"
But he refused to me the one remaining,
Fearful for his poor Shelah, still a boy.

What is a woman with none to suckle?
Twice widowed, I worked a desperate ploy:
I painted and veiled like a temple girl,
Where men will come to mount the holy nuns
And honor the god who cherishes seed.
Amorous Judah saw me there, disguised:

"I'll pay you a goat for a servicing, dear."

"Sir, I see no goats. Give me a pledge instead;
I'll keep your seal, until you make it good."

So Judah did the deed for his daughter-in-law;
He offered a kid, but gave me a son.
He paid no goat, though soon my belly showed,
And he, outraged, condemned me for my work:

"Our Tamar has played the whore, she must die."

"Father, here is your seal; where is my goat?"

Judah relented, ashamed and in the wrong,
And so was born Perez, forefather of David.
What men call sin the god can turn to good:
Playing whore, I gave the land a king.

What's the Point of Love Poetry?

"I don't know why you poets can't just say
What you mean," she scoffs, "instead of all this
Fiddle." I smile, disarmed by honesty:
"Why sing, when you can simply talk? Why pray,
When God already knows your deepest core?
Why make wine, when water is plentiful?
Why churn sweet cream? Just drink it warm and fresh.
Why roses, and chocolates? Why, indeed,
All these words, when the real business awaits?
Poems conceive what would have stayed unborn,
Being, my sweet, our language making love,
As now, in this very place, to that bright pink ear."

The Science of Love

(Homage to Richard Dawkins)

The essence of life is particulate,
The grandest fact you'll learn at school:
Deoxyribonucleic acid,
Earth's own self-replicating molecule.

Our genes are made of DNA;
We come and go, it's here to stay.
If genes had eyes, what they would see
Is other genes living through you and me.

We are their highway, our bodies the bus
To the generation replacing us.
From a gene's perspective your only use
Is to live long enough to reproduce.

This is the soul that will survive:
It's DNA that stays alive.

The Little Deaths

Why, my dear, had no one told me
That my every gush of love
Was rehearsal for an entrance
Into even kinder bed,
These lesser throes a preparation
For that last most potent shove
Into the lasting kind of dead?

As we who after grunting struggle
Recollect our final night:
First, a friction of resistance,
And a fear of letting go,
Then liquid slippings toward acceptance,
Soft upwellings of delight,
An effervescing after-glow,
And a sliding into light.

If I Were Dead

(After Carol Anne Duffy)

If I were dead
And my ashes spread
By caring friends,

Or drowned alone
And sunk like stone
To ocean's floor;

Were I heretic burned
And my ashes spurned
By every winnowing wind,

I swear your love
Would drag me dead
From some dank bed

And call me round,
Like Lazarus bound
In linen shroud,

To weep for joy,
To lip, and kiss,
And this, and this,
And God Himself
Would cry aloud.

The Sperm of Sudan Now Sleeps in Hope

(Sudan, the last male northern white rhino, died March 19, 2018, at age 45. There remain but two of his kind: his daughter Najin and grand-daughter Fatu.)

When Sudan died, his dozen caregivers wept,
Not just because he was magnificent
And they loved him, but that his long line now
Could end, forever. Quickly they withdrew
What little sperm remained in his wizened
Vesicles and froze it lovingly. Consider
Its infinite worth: fifty-five million
Years of urgent transmission culminate
In these precious droplets. Seed from others
Of his species now dead, also carefully
Preserved, quietly awaits its goal in
The body of young Fatu. What better hope
For the human heart itself than such love
For a dying kind not even ourselves?

Near Taos

The Santuario de Chimayo
Houses a small, and special, sacred place,
The Holy Dirt Room, beside the altar.
An alcove is lined with abandoned crutches
And prayers of thanks. Beyond it is the Room,
Where you will see a small hole in the floor,
Filled with ordinary sand. But only
To the eye. To the heart of faith, it is
A healing balm, drawing the troubled and
Hurt to its grace. This is what I saw there.

Amid a crowd of curious tourists
Were two men in worn and patched but clean clothes.
One of them spoke English, the other not.
"We are haulers of heavy loads," he said,
"Truck drivers, and jobs are scarce these days.
We came to Chimayo to pray for work."

These men kneeled, and with their hands gave sand
In scoops to the faithful who came after
Mass with their emptied plastic bags. "See,"
He said, smiling at them, "here we have work
Already, hauling holy dirt for you."

The Shearing of Clare by Francis

(On the evening of March 20, 1212, Palm Sunday, eighteen-year-old Chiara Offreducio of Assisi left her father's house and approached St. Francis at his chapel of the Porziuncola, praying him to help her live after the manner of the Gospel. There, he cut off her hair, signifying her vows as a nun, and dressed her in a coarse robe of repentance. He then escorted her to a convent of Benedictine nuns of San Paulo.)

What were you thinking, Francis, when you placed
Your hands upon that fragrant yellow hair?
What were you thinking, as you lifted
Those shining plaits from their scented home
And held them to the knife? Did you snatch them
First to your fasting mouth, to snuff the blossoms,
Verbena, or lavender, drifting from their strands,
And kiss them before ravishing that purest head?

What were you thinking, when with your own hands
You unwrapped her of perfumed silks, and robed
Her in glory of coarsest penitent's sack?

What were you thinking, when Clare fled her home
And came to you, alone and unafraid, for love,
Such love as our starved hearts can scarcely comprehend?
Not to be joined with you that day, but to
Be shorn of everything she had except
This love, to go unshod in all weathers,
To sleep unpillowed on God's stony floor,
And vow she'd cleave with never a spouse but the One.

Death Comes for St. Francis

Death came softly for you, Francis;
How could she otherwise? Nothing
That falls from the hand of God would shake you.

Our sister, death, came whispering in,
And kissed your fevered feet. She gently slipped
Into the soles, and cooled your calloused knees.
She unknotted the cramp in your thigh.

Then sad death paused, and sighed awhile,
Till slowly she rose, and groaned, and kissed
Your heart, to still its sweet beating forever.

So you had at last your soul's longing,
To yield up our poor brother the flesh,
That death become, as you knew she would,
Your friend, your sister, your love.

After Zika: The Aborted Fetus Comforts Her Grieving Mother

You were broken, and afraid
To see a face a virus made.

I had a shrunken, shapeless brain;
I would have lived in daily pain,

Then died too soon, to rend
Your heart and never let it mend.

To keep me from that pain,
You yielded me to God again.

You took on the agony
That would have come to me.

I thank you for your sacrifice.
Knowing you loved me
Enough to end me
Will suffice.

Sooner or Later, Delicate Death

There is an evening coming
Will bring you softest sleep,
Where a tree is leafing now
For shade from summer's heat.

A coverlid is waiting
Will warm in any storm.
Safe house is now prepared
Will keep from every harm.

Deepest earth is ready now
To be your bosom friend.
Nothing ever untoward
Could such attendants send.

Letter to God

Yes, I know, I'll be there soon,
I'm getting old. And if you
Really were here once—just supposing—
Then your own sweet birth was evidence
That love, at least, can bear some fruit.

When last you visited, some time
Ago, we killed you. Might you try
That again? Few here would be pleased,
And once bitten, twice shy, it's said.
Even we biters know this, so
I send no Magi gift, just this sprig
Of mint, plucked today— proof your world
Remains lovely beyond all words,
Even with you gone.

Bystander, near Jerusalem, Early Friday in Passover, 30 A.D.

I hear they caught him, that preacher of love
Your enemies and let them slap your face twice—
I don't get that. But still I went out to hear him,
He talked like one of us, with some good stories too.
I even had some fish his people passed around.
Not bad, though I prefer a bit more salt.
You wonder how they got them there so fresh,
Us being in the wilderness and all.
But I didn't take one of his dry barley loaves,
I kept waiting for that bread of life he
Talked about, but no one ever showed up
With it—wouldn't you know—and so I'm left
Sucking my teeth while he goes on about
The blessed piece-workers, and people who
Are poor in spirit, whatever that means.
I'm poor in coin myself, and I say blessed is
A full belly, with two greased lips to boot,
So I'd hear him out for his fish anytime.
Besides, there was something about his voice,
And his face when he talked, it made me feel—
Well, I don't know what it was. Clean, maybe.
Anyway, that devil Pilate has him now,
So I guess I'll never taste his bread of life.
I'd love to have a bit, with salt. I bet it's good.
I wonder if we'll ever see his face again.

About the Author

Until his retirement in 2007, Randel McCraw Helms was a professor of English at Arizona State University. His published works include a chapbook of poems, *Animal Prayers*, plus the books *Tolkien's World*, *Who Wrote the Gospels?*, *The Bible Against Itself*, and *Gospel Fictions*. He lives near Phoenix with his wife and cats.